MAKE A
MOVE
WHILE IT'S FRESH
UPON YOU

God Bless You

Mother Bobbie Pardue

Sincerely

PAMELA CARRIER

Pamela Carrier

PAMELA CARRIER

....

DEDICATION

To My God first for accepting me as I am. Thank You God for everything! This book is dedicated to the memory of my mother. My first love down here on earth, even while in her womb and out she has showed me so much love. The action of the word love was expressed in so many ways. You reign with me daily as a legacy that will never end; miss you and loving you mother forevermore until we meet again. I finally got my book out mother; kisses and hugs forever.

TABLE OF CONTENTS

ACKNOWLEDGEMENTS

To my children Rickey Jr. and Lisa and Christina, my grandchildren Rhaylen, Zachari'ah and Rickia. I can't leave out their mother Meccan, who has and is doing a great job in raising my grands. I praise God for letting me have you all in my life. Remember that you all cannot do anything without Christ. Continue to follow the steps where the Lord is leading you. Stay strong in the Lord and the power of His might. I'll never forget the memories of all the good times we've had together while raising you all. Especially watching you all at many settings rolling on the floor with laughter, then came the "shhhh" games, lol. Never stop loving on each other. I love you all forever more.

There are too many family and friends to name who have been there for me in my singleness, marriage and divorce through word, deed, finances etc. I just thank you all from the bottom of my heart. While sharing on social media to reach many souls, one of my church members texted and said, "Put it all in a book" and I thank her for acknowledging the call.

To the Leadership of many that were and are in my life thanks for the teaching of The Word of God that I have dwelling in my heart.

INTRODUCTION

There are many areas here to be covered while reading this book and coming up from living in poverty with not a cruel spot in my heart. But, remembering and knowing the Lord at a young age he was there all the time. "Let your conversation be without covetousness; and be content with such things as ye have; for he hath said, I WILL NEVER LEAVE THEE, NOR FORSAKE THEE." (Heb. 13:5) You have to train up your children while they are young, they will not depart. (Proverbs 22:6) "Train up a child in the way he should go: and when he is old, he will not depart from it."

While living in this world you have to prepare yourself mentally. Even though many do not like to read, I would encourage many to do so. Seeing what this book offers the good and the bad, you can conquer anything with what you have instilled in your mind, soul and body. Listen with a good ear. Discern the vibes from the one presenting the conversation to you. Reach out for greatness.

~1~

CHAPTER ONE
"YOUNGER DAYS"

My childhood was very interesting as I could remember. Mother kept us very neat and clean. My father died at an early age of 39 when I was only three years old. Knowing what I know now of what my mother went through brings me to the point that no matter what we went through we still have to trust God in all things. Mother raised us very well, all eight of her children graduated from high school some went to college and not one time did she have to go to jail to break us free from the system. When the holidays came around it was interesting but exciting because she did what she could do in making sure we had a gift or two under the tree. I remember going with her to stand in the welfare line to get commodities. At that time, I didn't know we were poor. We never went hungry our entire life of her raising us all eight by herself. One day she took me to the department store downtown called *Kress*. We didn't have a car so while everyone was asleep, she called a taxi to get there. While she was shopping there was this colorful lollipop that I wanted. After she paid for it and gave it to me, I was one of the happiest kids in the world. The lollipop was bigger than me. I was in the third or fourth grade. As the tears roll down my face right now, I am so grateful to have had a mother that made sure we stayed happy. Watching her cook for us was a joy. We may have eaten, eggs and rice with ketchup on it sometimes, mustard and rice, fried bologna sandwiches, peanut butter and jelly, our bellies were full. When it was time for us to take our bathes, we had to share the same water, but we stayed clean. Our hair was always on task. Eight children in a three bedroom it was very tight, but we all survived. I am thankful for her keeping us on point. So many times along with our neighbors, mother would make sure we got to school on time as they walked with us many days.

I loved going to school. Even though one day a boy punched me in my stomach and told me not to tell anyone and I didn't because I was shy; this is the first I've shared this. I saw him one time after I graduated from high school from a distance. But that's okay I'm sure he's reaped it already. He was one of the bad ones in school. While in elementary, middle, as well as high school I was tall, shy, and skinny. Pretty much staying to myself has always been my personality. Loving to see people happy was my enjoyment everywhere I went. Even when I wanted a part in their happiness, I was too shy to let them know. Eventually I gave it a try and realized that we cannot please and make everybody happy. Rejection is a hurting thing and the majority of my life rejection was trying to take over. Getting over it was very easy because I was already mentally prepared staying to myself. Don't push yourself into someone's life that you are not supposed to be in. It can really hinder you from your blessing. The height of 5'7 was leading me into wanting to play basketball while in middle school, but while in P.E. one day I got caught chewing gum and my teacher told me to get up and go trash the gum with my skinny legs, (didn't tell mother about that one either.) That stayed with me through my life. After that getting dressed for P.E. and even swimming; my grades went down in that class. Ending up in the choir was the fitted position for me to be in instead. Singing was another enjoyment for me. I went home one day and sang for my mother and she was so excited and told me to, "Sing it girl!" I sang *Amazing Grace.* Her words overlapped my discouragement. Words hurt and will destroy your dream if you let it.

So, don't allow what comes out of a person's mouth about you to quickly destroy you. "Life and death is in the power of the tongue." You are either going to speak life to your situation or death. Speak life. At the age of 13 still feeling insecure about my life at such a young age, we would visit a family members house and I came across one of them that touched me in an inappropriate way that scared me. She was younger than me but, bigger. It was like another situation approaching me, "Lord why, what's next? Why is she messing with me in that way? Will she hurt me if I tell or scream?" I just didn't know what to do. I didn't know how to talk to no one about anything. FIND SOMEONE TO TALK TO EARLY IN THE SITUATION BEFORE IT GETS WORSE IF YOU ARE BEING MISTREATED.

As frighten as I was no one knew. Talking to God about it protected me from her trying that again. People take advantage of small, tender people a lot. Now-a-day's they'll try you if you have low self-esteem etc. As we got older, it was never brought up when I was in that person's presence. But, in my mind I was like, why did you do that to me? In spite of the past I still treated that person with unconditional love. That same year two other people touched me inappropriately. Three times in one year but my virginity wasn't never taken. The secrets people hold when carrying it into their future can destroy them if they let it. But I didn't. Writing this is really helping me mentally and I pray it reaches someone else that is going through the same or similar situation. My understanding wasn't clear on why these things happened to me but, to this day I still trust God, overall. Vengeance is His already.

~2~

CHAPTER TWO
"EXPERIENCING THE WORLD"
I CORINTHIANS 15:53

Coming up in life no one shared with me about life, pregnancy, falling or being in love, not even relationship knowledge. While in elementary and middle school, my grades were great except for that P.E. class. That summer while preparing for high school, I started dating for the first time. I played with Barbie's and Ken dolls along with paper dolls up to the ninth grade. We went to the movies and that was my first kiss ever at the age of 15. It was pleasurable even though I didn't know what I was doing. Was I heading in the right direction? Not at all. So, I thought I was going to be with that one person of course, I fell in love right then and there for the rest of my life. Not knowing that it was my emotions that was causing me to lust for the things of this world that would lead me to destruction. He would shower me with gifts for every holiday and birthday even a just because gift. And I fell for it all. Eating out was over and above because I was so used to just eating only at home. So, my ninth-grade year wasn't going well at all. My grades went from A's to D's and E's. Who gets an "E" in physical education? Once he climaxed on the inside of me, my focus was no longer on my education. I never brought my grades back up to an "A." Modeling was my desire. The flesh was taking over my mental state of life. Letting my emotions direct my thoughts wasn't a pretty sight. In the midst of my emotions running wild, there went my virginity. That same night I saw my daddy in a vision even though I don't remember him. It's like he was telling me, don't make that move again. God works in mysterious ways. Why didn't I listen? Again, no teaching or spiritual guidance of any kind. You cannot live off of love. What happens next in my life was only shared with one friend. There were severe pains in my stomach that caused me to grab a hold of the wall while headed to the restroom. "Please, Lord not pregnancy?" I was in the tenth grade at that time. While in the restroom I started coughing uncontrollably. It was like I had a very bad cold. I grabbed what was in the medicine cabinet and drank it thinking, it would either ease the pain or the coughing. Reading the bottle, it read do not take if you think you are pregnant. Not minutes later, I flushed a clog out of me, and I knew it had to have been a baby. I cried. I went to school the next morning weak, and in pain bleeding like a water facet. I'm so glad that God kept me throughout the day it was an experience like no other. The miscarriage was another hurting part of my life. Sharing with him what happened to me would have been a waste but, God knows best. Life for me was crazy.

When realizing the relationship was one sided, this showed me you really can't trust anyone. Calls started coming in from other girls and women. I would have preferred being with my dolls than being introduced to those worldly things. Pressure and stress came. Walking the halls while girls would throw slangs at me about being with my boyfriend. They knew I stayed to myself. I kept walking to my classes like I never heard them. They were some "Big" girls. I was strong, taking the punches made me even stronger to not give into these petty situations. You don't have to stay in a relationship knowing you are being cheated on.

What was I thinking to stay in that drama of a relationship? Love makes you accept some unhealthy situations. Was it because it was my first one and only? Or was I afraid that no one else would want me? In my heart, until this day, I only commit to one person at a time. Again, taking advantage of someone is a cruel thing. Especially when they don't know what; or shall I say have been warned of what could take place in your life and that could damage you mentally if you let it. Dating this man at that time of my life is all I saw, was a man who was there for me in one way, but not the right way. I needed to be moving forward towards my future.

You live and learn. There was no covering or protection when we were out and about.

I remember he took me to the seawall just joy riding at that time. He saw a friend so he got out to speak to him and my window was down, and the friend pointed at me and asked him, "Is that who you are dating?" He burst out laughing. I looked like; he's not going to defend me from that laughter which wasn't a good one. Instead he just looked and smiled with the guy and kept talking. The feeling of making fun of me was hurtful for a long time. Did I ask him why didn't he stand up for me? No I didn't because I was afraid of the answer. If that happens to anyone I would encourage them to step up to the plate or talk to someone about what happened to you.

~3~

CHAPTER THREE
"MARRIAGE"

Nineteen eighty was when I graduated from High School. In the month of May of that same year I realized that I've been dating this same guy for three years. I never looked at another man while with him all those years. That month I dealt with girls and women calling my mother's phone; house phones only back then. Then while going to my next class they would talk to each other out very loud enough for me to hear what they were saying about my boyfriend at that time. "You were with who?" "Oh, okay then." Petty, knowing that I'm shy and stayed to myself and have very few friends.

They didn't care. With them being bigger and taller than me I kept walking. For one I had the ring on and they didn't. He put an engagement ring on me in

1979. So, why is this girl bothering us? Back then I didn't know about this book that I read about caring enough to confront, because I would have shared a few positive things with them. Confronting people doesn't make them tell the truth about the situation but at least you did your part in confronting whatever the situation was.

Giving up wasn't on my agenda but to stoop to negativity was never in my plans. When entering into a marriage you should not go into it with a closed mindset. Marriage is made for three people God, husband and wife. We must communicate and trust. Once you are in it keep those words before you both at all times. In living the single life protect or shall I say cover all areas; physically, mentally and spiritually. While moving forward towards your purpose, stand strong and be courageous!

Summer of 1980, I got pregnant and was still living with my mother. I told her and she didn't respond.

That was in July. When I shared it with my boyfriend at that time about the baby, he was like so what are you going to do? I was devastated. I am so glad that my decision was from God and not man to keep my little blessing. Confusion stepped in on what was to be my next step because, I brought the news to his parents and they were oh so excited. Well, my plans of becoming a model was put on hold at that moment. Even though I was still just a little bit shy. One of my campfire teachers called me to prepare me to go college right there in my hometown but, I didn't know how to tell her I was pregnant. The Dean said, "I'm going to take care of your tuition." I was in tears while crying in the closet on the phone with her. I didn't share that reasoning with her until 2017 of why I didn't accept her offer. She was a Dean at the college and an awesome woman. No matter what you go through when an opportunity is offered to you, run with it. I do believe that was a plan from God because, He knew that my mother couldn't assist in getting me off to college. She saw something in me that was ready to be birthed out at the time. Someone must see what's on the inside of you that can take you farther than you can imagine. Not too long after I spoke with his parents, wedding plans were being made by his mother. December rolled around I was about to become a wife at 19. Being interested in getting married wasn't in my view at all. And he wasn't interested in marrying me. As a matter of fact, my mother woke me up at 5:30p.m. and said Pamela you're about to be married in thirty minutes. I then got up looked in the mirror and said let's do this. Being five months pregnant, not having a place to call my own after the wedding yet, his not being interested in me was really weighing on me. I believe the wedding was a nice house wedding; she did an excellent job on it all but mentally I still wasn't ready. Just because you're pregnant does not give you the right to say "I do" to anybody if you're not ready. Many showed up for the occasion carrying gifts. I really appreciated her doing that and that's for sure. When the Pastor spoke the wrong name for us during the ceremony, I was like now I know this isn't right. But it wasn't my time just yet to be married. You have to speak up for yourself and stop letting others dictate your life. Even if it hurts both persons and people that are involved in the matter. Of course, there wasn't a honeymoon or anything. Not being happy was a bother in my mind that was taking control. We stayed with my in-laws for a while until their house next door was available to move in. When we finally did, I thought that would change matters for us to get more involved or intimate with each other. It didn't. I continued praying and enjoying carrying my little miracle on the inside of me. Even though I shared the movements of my baby alone, I was still excited about becoming a Mother. Waiting those four more months had me anxious to see my baby boy. When those Braxton Hicks were approaching me, I just knew that they were real labor pains. So, when they finally became real labor pains, my mother and auntie stayed patiently with me the whole time. My mother-in-law was working. Being in the labor room without my husband hurt me so bad. The embarrassment was horrible. Staying strong for yourself even makes you stronger. Those were the longest 22 hours of my life being in labor, but it was worth it all when my baby arrived. Such a joy overwhelmed my soul when I saw him. I covered him in prayer while carrying him and still to this day. Praise God! When I was home raising him was so easy because of the love God had given me to give him. My in-laws were a great help no doubt about that. Many times his grandmother would say her son instead of grandson. So, I'm wondering if this would bring some spunk to the marriage now that we have a son. Well I waited and it didn't. When I found out that marriage is a ministry, I prayed and worked on it more. But it takes two with both accepting God to lead it. Being that proverbs woman that I had finally read about is all I wanted to become. Feeling empty and lonely even though I was married was an unfair deal in my life. This puzzled me to know that I was with only one man and him not even appreciating that really had me in a shackled place. I loved on my baby boy so much morning, noon and night. I never enjoyed him together with his dad. Loving family is my passion. When my baby was nine months old there still was a distance between me and the daddy then him and my baby. One day he picked an argument because I asked about his where abouts. That didn't go well. He told me to move out. Oh my, really. I went back to my mother whose door is always open to everyone. My question was why did you put us out? He wanted to continue his single life even though he was married. I'm not writing to put no one down but, just a wake-up call to let someone know that you are way better than the way you are treated sometimes. While away I prayed constantly that God would open his eyes and heart to what was happening in his life as it pertained to his family. Prayers were answered, he came to pick us up after a couple of weeks. Well alright things are starting to look up like it should as a family. Even though we were not ready for the marriage, I still tried to make it work. God will answer prayer just for the asking but it may not be His will. He'll give us the desires of our heart. One day while being back at home, a neighbor kept tugging at my marriage. I saw it but not believing that this was happening. I ignored it. Then it happened again seeing something that wasn't pleasing in my sight and for sure not in God's sight. Really y'all, again I was afraid to say anything. I didn't want to have to go back and forth to my mother's house, one time was enough. A very discouraging scene. They both disrespected me and my house. Being submissive, it stayed in my view no matter what. Then finding out that her baby could have been my husband's baby around the same time that my first born came. It wasn't his. This was just too much that I was carrying and knowing what I know now I was strong back then and still am a strong woman today. I'm not going to say naïve. I didn't understand why would he want to cheat when I treated him like royalty? Cooked, cleaned, met his needs etc. But if no love is there that's the problem. But, the beginning of our relationship was love, so I thought. You cannot put your trust in no one. People will smile in your face and stab you in the back like nothing was ever between the two. Even if you think you can trust someone who you thought knows better is another thing. You just can't continue to let things happen in your life without taking heed to the issue. Ignoring the issue will also make matters worse. Don't let it slide. My prayers never stopped. One day he came home from work and said that he was going to church. While at my mother's house he called on one occasion and said that I'm coming back for my family when I have given my life to the Lord. So, we went as a family but, I still felt left out in more ways than one while attending the church. Going to church still will not make you or things right until you are a doer of His Word not just a hearer. I still wasn't getting the attention that I needed. Lord, what's a woman to do. We both received the gift of speaking in tongues, spread the good news to others, had Bible studies at our home, but where was the love in the home? We were going to church every time the door was open, but hearts were still closed to the things that needed to be taken care of at home. Smiling was all I had even though my insides were being crushed more and more. Unity is a powerful thing if you both are walking in it together. "When I thought we was, we were not." A praying woman will forever be on my agenda. I started examining myself and still did the wifely, motherly duties as I should. The devil didn't like us going to church. Worshipping and praising God under the same roof to me was awesome. Knowing in my heart that the people in church was ready for heaven. Not so. I caught more troubles in the church house than out. I'm not perfect, please believe me; but I'm striving for perfection.

Before long he decided to continue to move in the wrong direction, my heart was getting weaker by the day. My first born was five years old when I found out that our second child was growing on the inside of me. Nineteen months later our third child was born into this world. Okay God help me soon. Children are a blessing. This intimacy is making me feel like it is just for a seed to be planted there. I'm a dreamer for life it looks like.

One night I shared with him about three different dreams with three different women dealing with him. He denied them all. Prayer and more prayers, I prayed. Then one day after three years of dating, twelve years of marriage he wants out. So, there I was divorced with three children to raise by myself. Then he finally lets me know after all these years, I'M NOT IN LOVE WITH YOU. Then, oh yeah, the dreams you dreamed about me, they were all true. And I saw every one of those faces in my dream, Lord Jesus. While going through, what I went through I went to church just me and the kids. The Pastor passed by me one service and instead of saying how are you doing sister, instead he says, "Hey sister you got your divorce yet?" Wow he didn't encourage me at all. My face was stiff. Continuing to serve my God will keep me going to church. Plus, having a leader to encourage me to move forward is always a plus.

~4~

CHAPTER FOUR
"SINGLE LIFE"

What went wrong? Really nothing, it just wasn't that season for me to be married. Mentally the shutting down tried to hit me in my spirit. My joy was decreasing along with the huge smile. When after 15 years in total with someone who didn't love me but, lusted after me. (The smile is back) While raising my three children I realized that God got us. Without God, we can't do anything. His timing is way better than ours. Challenges came left and right but, the strength of the Lord approached me with, "I can do all things through Christ that strengthens me." He's my provider, way maker, He's omni-present at all times. God knows the needs of us all before we even ask. With my son being the oldest at the age of twelve, I was like "Jesus, please your word says you'll never leave or forsake us." I didn't want to mess up raising him being a woman, but it worked out great. Thanks to the Almighty. My son was very respectful back then with just me and he still is to this day. He's one very strong Father figure for his children. My girls were three and five and were used to just having me but wanted their daddy as well. Never say that divorce doesn't affect children because it does. The ability, strength, courage and knowledge to raise them being single reflected on me when realizing my mother raised eight children by herself when my daddy passed away. They had no idea of what was really happening being so young still wanting their daddy sometimes. You have to understand what a child could be going through. When we think they don't know what's happening some of them do. My kids started having allergies like none other. I walked around the house and realized that the mold in the house was getting worse. After moving my children out of the infested house there were no more problems with their breathing. Apartment hunting was a task, but it happened right on time. With God all things are possible. Seeing them happy made me happy. Preparing for life's responsibilities of PTA meetings, dancing, football games, graduations from elementary, middle then high school pleased me well, even though one parent was there. Once I attended their events surprising them put a smile on their face it was a fulfilling task.

So, I tried to date but it was a little hard because fifteen years of my life it was only one man. It brought mixed emotions, and some trouble, no focus to my life; you have to keep your focus no matter what you go through. It can leave you far behind in your past that you can't see what's in front of you. Meeting people, then sharing my situation became embarrassing. A pity party was in my view but, I overcame it quickly.

The crushing pain of facing or even thinking of what other men or women did to disrespect my marriage made me feel nauseous. The hurt tried to peek in every now and then. Even to the point that a church member knowing what I was going through approached me in a disrespectful way during this dating situation. Being single can be what you make of it. My first and second dates were very grievous, and a convicting situation; pleasing to the eye but leading to destruction. To this day my spirit corrects my flesh.

Inviting other men in my life with my children being so young, blinded me of not thinking or not protecting them for whatever may come out of these dating experiences. Think about your children's feelings. The "behind the scenes" sometimes will never be heard until after the fact if something were to go wrong; even in a mental capacity. Apologizing to my children as they became older made me feel like what a mother is supposed to feel like when correcting the mental issues when opening your mouth about the past.

With them seeing and hearing things that I didn't even see that was going on in these relationships made me more proud of them. I have some very wise and knowledgeable children that keep themselves intact mentally. Praying in the spirit a lot protected us all. You see sometimes the spirit guides you but, you continue to want to go your way that you would end up struggling longer than you should. In the midst of wanting to date, I should have gotten a divorce first because that's even worse, then you are committing adultery and fornicating at the same time. One day I was preparing for work and cleaned up before I left. Carrying a load of clothes up the stairs, I caught a severe pain in my stomach. I ignored it and continued getting ready for the day. I got to work, had to grab my stomach again and started feeling dizzy. After going to the restroom, I couldn't move for a minute. No one was in there to ask for help. I managed to get back to the office to let the secretary know that I needed to go home. At the moment the nurse of the school walked in and looked at me and I told her the same. She immediately said, "Take her straight to the hospital." I just wanted the pain that I was feeling to leave. She said my face was pale like I was losing blood. Fighting her to go home, the secretary took me to the ER instead. Upon arrival to the hospital while laying there with about five people looking at me not knowing what to do while in the ER because they had to wait for the doctor. I just wanted to die because that pain was real. They took different test, finally, he came in and that's all I remember until the next day and a half. When I had awakened, they told me that I had two and a half pints of blood sitting in my stomach. They had to take me straight to the operating room when the results came back. If I would have gone home, I would have died in ten minutes is what the doctor told me. Now remember I wasn't divorced yet. Saying that to say I would have died in my sins with a tubular pregnancy. But God had mercy on my soul. He kept me here to tell my story for His work, for His kingdom that I should be doing that had not been done. That sin of letting another man in me could have destroyed my life. God blocked that death spirit. You can't keep sinning when trying to reach the lost. Being single can drive you to death. Even though I wasn't lonely, I was approached and I'm guessing because of my vulnerable status which I didn't know what that meant at that time. It is important to reach out to the single men and women and this is something that should be taught to many. You don't have to give yourself away to everyone you meet because of your singleness. It's ok to be alone. After getting that person out of my life, peace came over me like still water. Timing is everything. But God's timing is everything and on point without a doubt. Never was I looking for someone to raise my children after their father left, I was just doing things not realizing I was doing it with no purpose behind it. You have to find and love yourself. Once you do that it will purposely take you to the next level of greatness that is awaiting you.

~5~

CHAPTER FIVE
"MOVING FORWARD"

Decision making is a plus when you're seeing that your life isn't moving and being at a standstill keeps you in a box. Boxes are made to keep things shut in with no movements. Until you open that box remove what's inside and do something with it, then your journey can begin. In doing that myself there were things that I know that was in there that was going to continue to help me with my children as well as others. I made sure my children were covered with love and compassion; getting out of that box helping others to feel more secure about themselves. Giving myself to God first of course then sharing life with many then stepping out of my comfort zone and pride wasn't easy. Receiving food stamps to survive for a minute due to the fact that my checks were not enough to feed, clothe and shelter my children; they helped along the way. Once pride was out that box, I took care of what needed to be done with gladness. Letting the government in on your life can have you looking back with another story to tell someone else about your journey in that area as well.

While working at my first real job and getting my first check and seeing the amount thinking how can I feed a family of four plus pay bills? So, from that point on I got into different marketing businesses to make ends meet. I didn't rely on the government to be my source for life. The struggle was and is real. Child support didn't kick in for years after that on and off. So, I couldn't depend on that either. Sometimes you have to let pride go because destruction is around the corner. Being obedient to the voice of God, which is His word, I started visiting a Word of Faith church. My Spirit was fed even more of the Word of God that was needed in my life. When God calls you please listen. The Word of God is so powerful and will speak life to you. While attending different

Theology classes kept me focused on life even more, I realized that speaking life to your situation brings life and manifestation of where you are supposed to be. During that season, I graduated from the class with my head up, saying, "There is work to be done. Don't just sit on what you have on the inside."

It's not about us but it is about the other person and building the Kingdom of God. Moving forward towards your goal is an active event that includes every part of your body. Meditation is mandatory as well.

Your light will shine brighter as you can see the light at the end of the tunnel. Your growth in the spiritual realm will elevate tremendously when you are focused on greatness. My next College class was coming up for me to attend. Attending Layman School of Ministry helped me spiritually. After graduating from that class, the University was in view. In 2005 Hurricane Rita hit Port Arthur bad. So, the class was put on hold due to us having to find shelter. We were in a shelter for six days praying and trusting God. Where are we going to lay our heads after we return back to our hometown? One of my cousins from Louisiana called and said, "Cousin I heard about the disaster there in Port Arthur." I told him where we were, and He said, "My home is open to your family." Believe me that church where we stayed for six days treated us with royalty but, it was time for us to go. Staying in Louisiana for ten days was truly a blessing. My cousin has a huge heart and I will always love him for that. When it was time to return to Port Arthur there was an offer then they changed their mind about us staying there. I prayed some more. There was nowhere for us to lay our head. Yes, I asked family and friends. I was rejected. But God had a plan. Upon having to resign from my job of working there for 13 years I was hurt; never look at the bad side. My youngest was in her senior year and wanted to graduate from there as well. That didn't happen either. I kept my smile and progressed to my next trial.

No matter what trials and tribulations came my way I continued to pray and trust God. Looking up to God with my faith is all I had. Transitions were a challenge. After our stay in Louisiana, we passed through Port Arthur to look at the damage that was done to the apartment. We grabbed what we could then headed to Houston. We had choices of hotels. The first one was definitely not a place to live for a while. There were roaches everywhere and holes in the wall. I looked at my son and was like no this isn't a descent place to lay our head. But where should we go? Maybe just for one night? As we were unloading the car, a lady passed by and said, "Hey ma'am you look like a child of the Most High God." She was leaving from the hotel with her things. I was like, "Yes ma'am." She said, "Come follow us we found a much nicer hotel." And it was. I was so excited because I was still looking out for my children even though they were older I covered them and will continue to do that. When we arrived at the nicer hotel it was very pleasing in my sight. It was like from rags to riches. Our stay was very nice. There was no stove but a small refrigerator, our finances became a struggle with eating out a lot and buying food that goes in the microwave. Believe me buying gas was not fun. Houston is so big, and we had to go far from where we were when wanting anything because we didn't know anyone that could lead us to where we wanted to go. Traveling to get food, drinks and clothing etc. brought tears to my heart. Shedding tears some sad, some happy when no one was looking, God was letting me know that this too shall pass.

We found a Church home in the area where we were sheltered, I was so thankful for that because I'm lost when I'm not in the house of the Lord. I had my praise on every time the door was open; then came finding a school for my youngest daughter who was a senior to attend. An employee of the hotel did help us in that area of need. It was hard because she wanted to graduate from her school in Port Arthur. So, in trying to fulfill her request one of her friend's mother opened her door for her to come there to finish her year out. In my heart knowing she's my responsibility until she is of age, I didn't want her to go back to let someone else raise her. Well, that didn't work out confusion set in and she was back with me and I was very happy for that. God knows our hearts and He knows exactly what is best for us. I located a school for her to attend since we were new to the area it worked out fine for her. My oldest daughter was patient in applying for jobs while in the hotel. The next step was apartment shopping. My son found his apartment first. I was thankful for that. After 43 days in the hotel I found an apartment 10 minutes from her school. What a blessing that was. Education is a plus no matter the circumstances. With her personality she fit in perfect at the school. After I was settled with getting everyone in place, job hunting was in my view. It was time for me to go back to work after being off a year. When in a new city I thought it was going to be very hard for me to find a job. But it wasn't. I started with a Head Start program 20 minutes from the house. It lasted nine months but I was thankful for that. That meant I had to have my daughter to ride the school bus because I had been taking her myself. I was very protective of my children no matter where I was and how old they were while still in my care. I wanted to make sure that they could look back and say that their mother did the best that she could in making sure that we stayed on the right track. The area that we were in was not that pleasing.

I continued praying on a nonstop basis for them all while here in Houston. An incident took place while my daughter was walking from the bus stop that I know without praying something could have happened. The door was open that one of her classmate's mother offered to start coming to pick her up for school and there went another answered stress free prayer. He's always on time. I had my car broken into one time while living in that area then they tripled my water bill and it was almost a house note. "Okay, God what's next?" But these trials of my faith made me hold on and to never give up. God's Word says, "He'll supply all our needs according to His riches in Glory through Christ Jesus." He did just that. Tribulations in this life will come because you stay where you are or know that you can move forward and learning while in it. I did stay there a little longer after my daughter did graduate from High School. Upon moving to another apartment since they wanted me to pay all that money for all the unnecessary utilities, God opened the door to another apartment that took me in very quickly because the last place had given me a three day eviction notice even though it was not my fault. They ordered me to go to court and I won, but God. Often times we don't understand what happens at that moment that's why His word says to not lean on our own understanding. So, there I was fighting a battle which wasn't mine to fight. I still knew that I shall remain a winner. My car payment was one month behind. My next source of income was going to come in the next two weeks. At this time excitement came upon me because, I would finally have a car title in my name. Well a "so called" friend turned my name in for the people to come pick up my car. I stepped outside at a friend's house and my car said, "Look for me." Then I tried getting it back, but they wanted triple the payment. You have to be careful when people say they are your friend because jealousy can set in and you not even knowing that those kind of feelings were there.

There I was with no car here in Houston and it was very hard. So, Metro became my friend for 9 long years. I never complained. Many times, while walking down the street with no money for a bus card even, I would still thank God because it could have been worse. I would look up and say, "Lord what is my purpose for being here with hardly nothing to comfort my needs?" Then He reminded me your needs have been met every time you were in distress. Well, what about me walking these roads alone with me not knowing anyone to communicate with. You are never alone because I have never left you and I don't sleep, so your communication with me is available 24/7. Why are these people shouting at me while I'm walking a 15 minute walk from the store saying ugly words at me God? He said, "Their words can never harm you but, my word will take you farther than theirs." Enough said. Thank You Lord for always being there for me no matter what side of the world I am on. I can truly say my steps are ordered by the Lord.

When this one guy passed by me while walking from the store one day because I didn't have money that day for the bus, carrying four bags he said this, "Hey you want a ride?" I didn't answer. Then he said, "Why your boyfriend got you walking down the street as beautiful as you are?" I didn't answer. Then he said, "That's good for you that's why you are walking." And he sped on down the road. I'm so thankful for God keeping me through everything that I am and shall go through while here on earth. The enemy tries to discourage me in many ways. Pushing through it all makes me stronger. Did I like some of my choices throughout my life, no I didn't. Sometimes I didn't stay focused just doing things just because can mess you up if you continue with the same mind frame. Let the Lord be your guide.

To Vote Text

Made in the USA
Monee, IL
13 September 2020